CARMELO ANTHONY

John A. Torres

NEW YORK

7

Mitchell Lane
PUBLISHERS

P.O. Box 196
Hockessin, Delaware 19707
Visit us on the web: www.mitchelllane.com
Comments? Email us: mitchelllane@mitchelllane.com

Mitchell Lane
PUBLISHERS

Printing   1   2   3   4   5   6   7   8   9

A Robbie Reader Biography

Aaron Rodgers	Drake Bell & Josh Peck	LeBron James
Abigail Breslin	Dr. Seuss	Mia Hamm
Adrian Peterson	Dwayne "The Rock" Johnson	Michael Strahan
Albert Einstein	Dwyane Wade	Miley Cyrus
Albert Pujols	Dylan & Cole Sprouse	Miranda Cosgrove
Alex Rodriguez	Eli Manning	Philo Farnsworth
Aly and AJ	Emily Osment	Raven-Symoné
Amanda Bynes	Emma Watson	Roy Halladay
AnnaSophia Robb	Hilary Duff	Selena Gomez
Ashley Tisdale	Jaden Smith	Shaquille O'Neal
Brenda Song	Jamie Lynn Spears	Story of Harley-Davidson
Brittany Murphy	Jennette McCurdy	Sue Bird
Carmelo Anthony	Jeremy Lin	Syd Hoff
Charles Schulz	Jesse McCartney	Taylor Lautner
Chris Johnson	Jimmie Johnson	Tiki Barber
Cliff Lee	Johnny Gruelle	Tim Lincecum
Dakota Fanning	Jonas Brothers	Tom Brady
Dale Earnhardt Jr.	Jordin Sparks	Tony Hawk
David Archuleta	Justin Beiber	Troy Polamalu
Debby Ryan	Keke Palmer	Tyler Perry
Demi Lovato	Larry Fitzgerald	Victoria Justice
Donovan McNabb		

Library of Congress Cataloging-in-Publication Data
Torres, John A.
 Carmelo Anthony / by John A. Torres.
    p. cm. — (A robbie reader)
 Includes bibliographical references and index.
 ISBN 978-1-61228-333-3 (library binding)
 1. Anthony, Carmelo, 1984– —Juvenile literature. 2. Basketball players—United States—
Biography—Juvenile literature. I. Title.
 GV884.A58T66 2013
 796.323092—dc23
 [B]
                                                                                    2012028099
eBook ISBN: 9781612284019

ABOUT THE AUTHOR: John A. Torres is an award-winning journalist and sports columnist for *Florida Today* newspaper. He has covered many sporting events, including the 2012 All-Star game that featured Carmelo Anthony. Torres is a published author with more than 50 books to his credit. Learn more about him on www.johnatorres.com and follow him @johnalbertorres on Twitter.

PUBLISHER'S NOTE: The following story has been thoroughly researched and to the best of our knowledge represents a true story. While every possible effort has been made to ensure accuracy, the publisher will not assume liability for damages caused by inaccuracies in the data, and makes no warranty on the accuracy of the information contained herein. This story has not been authorized or endorsed by Carmelo Anthony.

TABLE OF CONTENTS

Words in **bold** type can be found in the glossary.

Carmelo Anthony catches a pass and looks to shoot against the Boston Celtics during the 2011 NBA Playoffs.

Epic Night

On April 19, 2011, Carmelo Anthony's new team, the Knicks, were in a bind.

The Knicks were making their first playoff appearance in 10 years and were suddenly shorthanded against the powerful Boston Celtics. Star players Amar'e Stoudemire and Chauncey Billups were hurt and could not play.

Carmelo, already regarded as one of the top five basketball players in the NBA, knew his teammates would be looking to him to provide points for the Knicks. In an ESPN press conference after the game, his coach Mike D'Antoni, recalled telling Carmelo "we need you to carry us tonight."

Carmelo Anthony drives against number 7 Jermaine O'Neal of the Boston Celtics in Game Three of the Eastern Conference Quarterfinals in the 2011 NBA Playoffs at Madison Square Garden in New York City.

The *New York Daily News* called his efforts that night "epic." Carmelo scored an incredible 42 points against one of the best defensive teams in the league. On top of that he also grabbed a whopping 17 rebounds, blocked two shots and passed out six **assists**. He was a one-man team.

"I tried to carry the team not only scoring, but doing other things," Carmelo told reporters after the game, according to *The Record*. Carmelo scored with jump shots, with layups, with dunks after spinning his way to the basket. He simply could not be stopped.

Boston superstar Kevin Garnett **marveled** at Carmelo after the game. "I thought some of the shots he made were just incredible," Garnett told ESPN.

His efforts, heroic as they were, simply were not enough to beat the former world champs. The Celtics won the game 96-93 and would go on to win the series and eliminate the Knicks from the playoffs. But for Knick fans everywhere, Carmelo's incredible game provided them with hope for things to come.

Carmelo's mother Mary was a big positive influence in his life. Here they are together following the 2003 NCAA Championship Game.

Growing Up

Carmelo Kiyan Anthony was born on May 29, 1984. Carmelo was named after his father, who died when Carmelo was only two years old. His father was from Puerto Rico. His mother Mary is African-American. Carmelo grew up as the youngest of four children, including one sister, Michelle, and two brothers, Wilford and Justice.

The family was very poor and lived in a housing project in Brooklyn, New York. The family moved to Baltimore, Maryland, when Carmelo was eight years old.

He lived in an area where crime, violence, and drugs were common. Carmelo wanted to stay away from those things and so he started playing sports instead. His favorite game to play? Basketball, of course.

Carmelo's mother is a deaconess, a woman who works with the church to help others. His mother had a big influence on Carmelo. "When I was six, everything in my household had God in it," he told *Esquire* in 2011. He says that God has always been important to him.

Carmelo attended Towson Catholic High School where he played on the school's basketball team. Carmelo was always pretty tall. When he was a **sophomore** (SOF-uh-mohr) in high school he was already six feet tall. But he experienced a growth spurt during the summer and by the time he was a junior, Carmelo was six foot, five inches tall.

He had already been a very good basketball player. But now that he was taller, Carmelo was a scoring machine. No one could stop him. During that junior year in high school, Carmelo scored 23 points and grabbed 10 rebounds per game.

The National Basketball Association, or NBA, used to let teams draft players right from high school. Carmelo thought he would be playing in the NBA after graduation, but pro **scouts** said he wasn't strong enough. He would have to play college basketball first.

The problem was that he had started to skip classes, and was getting bad grades in school. Syracuse University in New York—a school with a strong basketball team— wanted Carmelo to play for them, but he would have to improve his grades.

Carmelo's mother, Mary, decided that a change of scenery might help her son get back on track. She took him out of Towson Catholic High School and enrolled him in Oak Hill Academy. Carmelo got his grades up, played great basketball and was ready for college.

Carmelo is all smiles as he poses with the NCAA Men's Basketball Championship trophy after a Syracuse win over Kansas on April 7, 2003.

National Champion

Carmelo's college career did not last long, but it was **memorable**. He enrolled at Syracuse in 2002 and instantly became the main focus of the school's basketball team. He was only a **freshman** playing with and against players who were often older and stronger. But it didn't matter. Carmelo played great. He averaged 22.2 points per game and 10 rebounds. That was more rebounds than any other freshman playing Division I basketball. Carmelo led his team in scoring and rebounding while averaging more than 36 minutes of playing time per game.

The best college teams in the country compete in what is known as the NCAA Tournament. Syracuse qualified for the tournament and continued beating teams until there were only four left: the "Final Four." Syracuse had never won the tournament before, and now they were getting close.

But first the Orangemen would have to beat the University of Texas, the top-ranked team in the tournament. Carmelo's 33 points helped Syracuse to pull ahead with a big lead. But Texas slowly chipped away at the lead, and with about one minute left, Syracuse was ahead by only four points. In the last 60 seconds, Carmelo and his team **dominated** and finally won 95-84, earning a spot in the championship game against the University of Kansas.

Carmelo seemed to thrive on the big stage—the bigger the game got, the better he played. He got on the court against Kansas and did his thing, scoring 20 points and 10 rebounds. Syracuse had built another good first half lead of 11 points. In the second half, however, Kansas came back and the score was tight through the rest of the game. In the final seconds, Syracuse led 81-78. But Kansas's Michael Lee had the ball, and he threw for a three point shot to tie the game. Lee's shot was

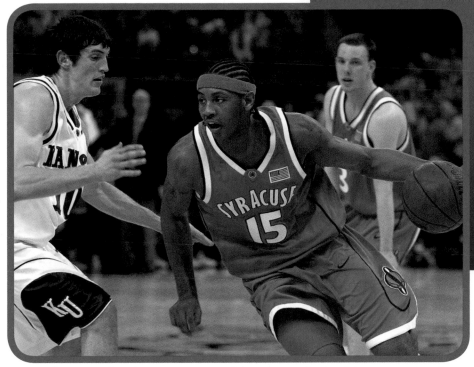

Carmelo proved to be an unstoppable scorer during his one and only season at Syracuse University.

blocked with less than a second to go, and Carmelo and his teammates became national champions.

Years later, his college coach Jim Boeheim, told *The Syracuse Post-Standard* that what made Carmelo great was that he just wanted to win and never cared about how many points he scored. "He thought about winning the national championship," Boeheim said. "He focused on that. He didn't try to score points, he just tried to play basketball."

Carmelo shows his athleticism as he rebounds and shoots in one motion during a National High School All-Star Game at Madison Square Garden in New York.

CHAPTER FOUR

NBA!

Carmelo's college coach could see his talent, and told him he that he was going to be an NBA star. So, after only one year of college basketball, Carmelo decided he was going to enter the draft to be selected to play for an NBA team. In the draft, the best player in the country is usually chosen first.

Carmelo had already won a college championship and had proven to be one of the best college players in the country. During the summer of 2002, before he started college, he had also played basketball as a member of the U.S. Men's Junior National Team. He earned **valuable** (VAL-yoo-uh-buhl) experience playing against international competition. As usual,

Carmelo led his team in scoring, averaging 15.6 points per game.

It was time for a new challenge: the NBA.

The Cleveland Cavaliers had the first pick of the 2003 draft and they chose a high school kid named LeBron James, who turned out to be a great player. The Detroit Pistons chose Darko Milicic with the second pick. But no one was happier than the team with the third pick of the draft: the Denver Nuggets.

The Nuggets wasted no time in selecting Carmelo Anthony. At 19, he was one of the youngest players in the league.

Carmelo scored 12 points in his first game, but scored a whopping 30 points in only his sixth game. He quickly emerged as one of the league's best scorers using a wide range of flashy moves. It was hard to guard Carmelo because he was able to score from the outside as well as drive to the basket. He mainly played small forward but sometimes played power forward or point guard. He even scored 41 points later that season in a game against the

Carmelo poses in his new Denver Nuggets home uniform after being selected in the first round of the NBA draft.

Seattle SuperSonics (who later became the Oklahoma City Thunder).

Although LeBron James won the **Rookie** (ROOK-ey) of the Year award that year, Carmelo was **integral** (IN-ti-gruhl) in turning the Nuggets into a respectable NBA team in only a year. Before Carmelo arrived, the team had posted a terrible 17-65 record. The team finished 43-39 during his rookie season.

Carmelo enjoys an on-court rivalry and off-court friendship with superstar LeBron James.

Carmelo gives back to his community in may ways, including donating $1.5 million to help build the Carmelo Anthony Youth Development Center, which was opened on December 14, 2006. On the day the Center was opened, Carmelo received a portrait in his honor from Najee Rollins (far right), and Raymond Robinson (right) of The Crossroads School.

By the end of his first year in the NBA, Carmelo was a star with a lot of money. But he never forgot where he came from and he became very involved with several charities. He helped provide poor families with Christmas gifts in Denver, and in Baltimore he opened a youth center to help keep kids active with sports, art, and education. He even donated $3 million to Syracuse University to help build a new basketball center.

During the 2008 Olympic Games, Carmelo played for the U.S. Men's Basketball Team. In the final game, the team defeated Spain 118-107 to win the gold medal.

Play to Win

In 2004, Carmelo won a bronze medal with the U.S. Men's Basketball Team at the **Olympics** (oh-LIM-pix). That was also the year he met his future wife, television personality La La Vazquez. He played in the Olympics again in 2008 where he helped the Americans win the gold medal. Over the years, he has established himself as one of the league's best scorers and is now regarded as one of the top five players in the NBA.

With Carmelo on board, the Nuggets went to the playoffs for seven straight seasons.

In 2007, Carmelo and La La had a son together, named Kiyan Carmelo, and after a five year engagement, they were married in 2010.

Carmelo, wife La La, and son Kiyan attend the unveiling of Carmelo Anthony's Boost Mobile Billboard in Manhattan.

Less than a year later, on February 22, 2011, Carmelo was traded to the Knicks, who gave up several key players in exchange. Carmelo was now on a mission to help the Knicks win a championship. In his first game with the Knicks, he scored 27 points.

"It's still **surreal** (SUH-reel) to me to wake up in the morning and seeing the New York Knick uniform hanging on the door and seeing the blue and orange," Carmelo told the *New York Post* a week after being traded.

The Carmelo trade paid off instantly for the Knicks, who made the playoffs for the first time since 2004. The team lost in the first round, but looked forward to the future when Carmelo would be teamed up with players like Jeremy Lin, Amar'e Stoudemire and Tyson Chandler for another shot at the championship.

Carmelo was voted as a starter for the annual All-Star in 2012, his fifth all-star game as a pro.

Carmelo Anthony appears to be a man who has it all. He's happily married, involved in charity work, and he's a great professional

New York Knicks owner James Dolan introduces new player Carmelo Anthony at a press conference at Madison Square Gardens on February 23, 2011.

basketball player with a gold medal. But Carmelo's dream is to win the NBA Championship ring—and even that may not satisfy the hard-working player.

"My best moment is still coming," he told *Esquire.* "I'll never be satisfied with just one ring."

CAREER STATISTICS

Year	Team	G	MIN	FGM	3PM	FTM	REB	AST	STL	BLK	TO	PTS
03-04	DEN	82	2,995	624	69	408	498	227	97	41	247	1,725
04-05	DEN	75	2,608	530	42	456	426	194	68	30	224	1,558
05-06	DEN	80	2,941	756	37	573	394	216	88	42	218	2,122
06-07	DEN	65	2,486	691	40	459	391	249	77	23	234	1,881
07-08	DEN	77	2,806	728	58	464	571	259	98	39	253	1,978
08-09	DEN	66	2,277	535	63	371	450	222	75	24	199	1,504
09-10	DEN	69	2,634	688	59	508	454	222	88	30	209	1,943
10-11	DEN	50	1,774	437	42	343	382	140	43	31	142	1,259
10-11	NYK	27	977	247	53	164	181	81	25	15	64	711
10-11	--	77	2,751	6843	95	507	563	221	68	46	206	1,970
11-12	NYK	55	1,876	441	68	295	344	200	62	24	144	1,245
Career		646	23,374	5,677	531	4,041	4,091	2,010	721	299	1,934	15,926

(G = Games played, MIN = Minutes played, FGM = Field goals made, 3PM = Three-pointers made, FTM = Free throws made, REB = Rebounds, AST = Assists, STL = Steals, BLK = Blocks, TO = Turnovers, PTS = Points)

CHRONOLOGY

1984 Carmelo Kiyan Anthony is born on May 29 in Brooklyn, New York.

2000 Grows to be six foot, five inches tall while he is still in high school.

2003 Leads Syracuse University to the NCAA championship in March. In June he becomes the third player chosen in the NBA draft when he is selected by the Denver Nuggets.

2004 Sets a Denver team record for rookies when he scores 41 points in a game in March. He plays for the U.S. Olympic Men's Basketball Team, winning a bronze medal in Athens, Greece.

2007 Son Kiyan Carmelo is born in March.

2008 Plays for the U.S. Olympic Men's Basketball Team and this time helps the squad win the gold medal in Beijing, China.

2010 Marries his longtime girlfriend, La La Vazquez, on July 10.

2011 Is traded to the New York Knicks in February.

2012 In February, plays his first NBA All-Star game as a Knick.

FIND OUT MORE

Books, Articles, and DVDs

Anthony, Carmelo. *Carmelo Anthony: It's Just the Beginning.* Kirkland, WA: Positively for Kids, 2004.

Carmelo's Way (DVD), New Video Group, November 2010.

Hoblin, Paul. *Carmelo Anthony (Playmakers).* Minneapolis: Abdo Publishing Company, 2012.

Torsiello, David P. *Read About Carmelo Anthony (I Like Sports Stars!).* Berkeley Heights, NJ: Enslow Elementary, 2011.

Whitaker, Lang. "Carmelo Anthony: 'I'm back, baby.'" *Slam,* November 2009.

Works Consulted

@carmeloanthony. Twitter. http://twitter.com/#!/carmeloanthony

Adamek, Steve. "That's Two Bad." *The Record,* April 20, 2011.

Associated Press. "Celtics go up 2-0 on Knicks despite Carmelo Anthony's 42 points." ESPN.com, http://espn.go.com/nba/recap?id=310419002

Berman, Marc. "Carmelo 'comfortable' with Knicks after win over Heat." *New York Post,* February 28, 2011.

Carmelo Anthony Foundation: Carmelo Anthony. http://www.carmelocares.org/Carmelo

"Carmelo Anthony." NBA.com. http://www.nba.com/playerfile/carmelo_anthony/bio.html

Fussman, Cal. "Carmelo Anthony: What I've Learned." *Esquire,* January 2005.

Isola, Frank. "Amar'e Stoudemire hurt, Carmelo Anthony scores 42 as Knicks lose to Boston Celtics, trail series 2-0." *The New York Daily News,* April 19, 2011. http://articles.nydailynews.com/2011-04-19/sports/29473135_1_amar-e-stoudemire-knicks-paul-pierce

FIND OUT MORE

"Jim Boeheim reflects on 2003 NCAA title, Carmelo Anthony." *The Syracuse Post-Standard,* November 1, 2011.

Johnson, K.C. "Which Team Came Out Ahead in Anthony Trade?" *Chicago Tribune,* February 24, 2011. http://articles.chicagotribune.com/2011-02-24/ sports/chi-110224-four-corners_1_anthony-trade-timofey-mozgov-knicks

Kiszla, Mark. "Kiszla: Stan's Nod Needed for a Trade." *The Denver Post,* January 14, 2011. http://www.denverpost.com/kiszla/ci_17092757

Wojnarowski, Adrian. "'Melo Sees Good, Bad of Garden Life." *Yahoo! Sports,* February 24, 2011. http://sports.yahoo.com/nba/news? slug=aw-anthonyknicks022411

On the Internet

Carmelo Anthony Foundation
http://www.carmelocares.org/main.asp
Carmelo Anthony Official Web Site
http://www.thisismelo.com
NBA.com: Carmelo Anthony
http://www.nba.com/playerfile/carmelo_anthony/

GLOSSARY

assist—To help another person. In basketball, an assist is awarded to the player whose pass results in his or her teammate scoring a basket.

dominate—To control completely.

freshman—A student in his or her first year of high school or college.

integral (IN-ti-gruhl)—An important part of something bigger.

marveled—Looked at with wonder or admiration.

memorable—Something that will be remembered for a long time.

Olympics (oh-LIM-pix)—Games that are held every four years where countries from all over the world compete in sporting events.

rookie (ROOK-ey)—A person who is new at something. In sports it refers to a player in their first year.

scout—An expert who travels the country searching for the best new players.

surreal (SUH-reel)—An experience that does not seem real.

sophomore (SOF-uh-mohr)—A student in his or her second year of high school or college.

valuable (VAL-yoo-uh-buhl)—Worth a lot, important.

INDEX